World Book's Learning Ladders

Plants Around the World

WORLD
BOOK

a Scott Fetzer company
Chicago
www.worldbookonline.com

WORLD BOOK

233 N. Michigan Avenue
Chicago, IL 60601
U.S.A.

For information about other World Book publications, visit our Web site at
http://www.worldbookonline.com or call 1-800-WORLDBK (967-5325).

For information about sales to schools and libraries, call 1-800-975-3250 (United States);
1-800-837-5365 (Canada).

Library of Congress Cataloging-in-Publication Data

Plants around the world.
    p. cm. -- (World Book's learning ladders)
  Summary: "Introduction to plants using simple text,
illustrations, and photos. Features include puzzles and
games, fun facts, a resource list, and an index"--Provided
by publisher.
  Includes index.
  ISBN 978-0-7166-7742-0
  1. Plants--Juvenile literature. I. World Book, Inc. II.
Series: World Book's learning ladders.
  QK49.P545 2011
  580--dc22
                                                    2010022378

World Book's Learning Ladders
Set 2 ISBN: 978-0-7166-7746-8

Printed in China by Shenzhen Wing King Tong Paper Products Co., Ltd.
Shenzhen, Guangdong
1st printing December 2010

Editorial
  Editor in Chief: Paul A. Kobasa
  Associate Manager, Supplementary Publications:
    Cassie Mayer
  Writer: Shawn Brennan
  Researcher: Cheryl Graham
  Manager, Contracts & Compliance
  (Rights & Permissions): Loranne K. Shields

Graphics and Design
  Manager: Tom Evans
  Coordinator, Design Development and Production:
    Brenda B. Tropinski
  Photographs Editor: Kathy Creech

Pre-Press and Manufacturing
  Director: Carma Fazio
  Manufacturing Manager: Steven Hueppchen
  Production/Technology Manager: Anne Fritzinger

Photographic credits: Cover: © Comstock Images/Getty Images; WORLD BOOK illustration by
Q2A Media; Shutterstock; p3, p4, p8, p10, p14, p18, p21, p23, p27, p28, p29: Shutterstock; p6,
p20: Alamy Images; p11, p19: iStockphoto; p14, p16: Dreamstime; p30: Photodisc.

Illustrators: WORLD BOOK illustration by Q2A Media; WORLD BOOK illustration by Darrell
Wiskur; WORLD BOOK illustration by James Teason

What's inside?

This book tells you about lots of different kinds of plants—from your backyard to the steamy rain forests of Madagascar. You'll learn about what plants need to survive—and how they help *us* survive.

What is a plant?

Plants are living things that grow in almost every part of the world. Plants grow on mountaintops, in oceans, in deserts, and in snow-covered areas. Some plants tower over people and animals. Others are so tiny that they can hardly be seen!

Plants can have long lives. The oldest trees are California's bristlecone pines. Some of these trees are between 4,000 and 5,000 years old!

Most **roots** grow under the ground. They hold the plant in the soil. They also take in water and minerals that the plant needs to grow.

The **stem** holds up the plant and carries food to all parts of the plant.

Flowers grow from buds along the stems of a plant. Seeds are made inside the flowers.

Leaves make food for the plant.

It's a fact!

The tallest trees are California's redwoods. Some are several stories taller than the Statue of Liberty!

5

How do plants grow?

All living things need energy to grow. Animals get energy from the food they eat, such as plants and other animals. But plants make their own food from sunlight. Most plants also need water, air, and soil to grow. The big picture shows the growth of a bean plant.

Water lilies can live with most of their parts underwater. The plant's beautiful flowers grow on long stalks that rise from the mud bottom.

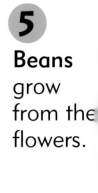

5
Beans grow from the flowers.

1

Plants begin life as a **seed**. A **seedling** grows from a seed.

2

The **root** grows down. The **stem** breaks through the soil.

3

The **buds** become the first **leaves**.

4

The stem grows upward. Leaves grow and **flowers** begin to bloom.

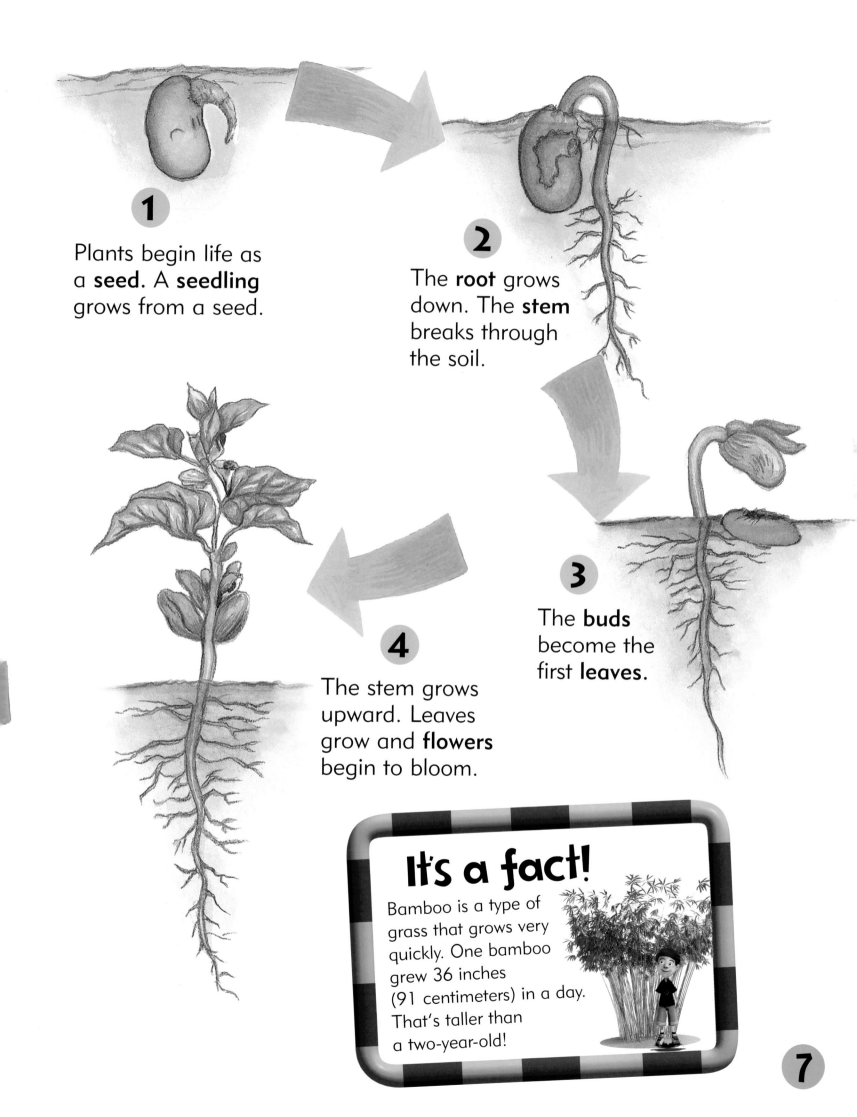

It's a fact!

Bamboo is a type of grass that grows very quickly. One bamboo grew 36 inches (91 centimeters) in a day. That's taller than a two-year-old!

Tree

Trees are the largest of all plants. Some trees are taller than a 30-story building! Many trees live longer than other plants. Some trees grow fruits, nuts, or flowers. The big picture shows an apple tree.

It's a fact!

The world's largest tree is the General Sherman Tree, in Sequoia National Park in California. There is enough wood in the tree to build a box that could contain the largest ocean liner!

In places that have cold winters, the leaves of many kinds of trees turn bright colors in the fall. Then the leaves fall off. New leaves grow back in the spring.

The apples are the **fruit** of the tree. Seeds are inside the fruit.

Leaves collect sunlight. Plants make food from sunlight.

Branches are high up in a tree.

Bark protects the tree's stem, roots, and branches. Wood is under the bark.

A tree has a large woody stem called a **trunk.** A tree trunk can stand by itself.

9

Grass

Grasses grow in almost every environment. There are many different kinds of grass. Wheat, oats, and corn are types of grass plants that provide food for people and animals. Grass is an important plant on a farm.

Bamboo is a type of woody grass. China's giant pandas live in bamboo forests and eat bamboo shoots.

Wheat is a type of cereal grass. Foods like bread, pasta, and breakfast cereals are made from wheat.

A **machine** called a combine has sharp blades that cut down tall grasses.

Animals that eat grass are called **grazers**.

Rice is one of the world's most important food crops. It is a grass that grows in shallow water.

When the top of the grass is cut off, the grass will begin to grow new **shoots** lower down on the stem.

11

In your backyard

There are many kinds of plants all around us. There may be all sorts of plants in your own backyard or in a nearby park. What kinds of plants do you see here?

12

What part of the plant are the bees visiting?

Words you know

Here are some words that you learned earlier. Say them out loud, then try to find the things in the picture.

trunk   flower   leaves
branch   stem   grass

13

Which things in the picture are helping plants grow?

Fern

Ferns are green plants that have no flowers. They grow in damp, shady areas. Ferns have some of the most beautiful leaves in the plant world. Some ferns look like mosses and are no larger than the tip of your thumb. Others look like trees and grow to more than 65 feet (20 meters) tall!

A fern's large leaves are called **fronds.**

Some kinds of ferns have long, lacy leaves made up of tiny **leaflets.**

Tiny balls under a fern's leaf contain **spores.** The spores grow into new fern plants.

Mosses are related to ferns. They make soft, thick mats on rocks or soil or at the bottom of a tree.

A young **fern leaf**
is coiled like the
top of a violin.

15

Cactus

Ouch! Watch out for a cactus's prickly spines! Most cactuses grow in hot, dry places in North and South America. But some grow in rain forests and on mountains. Some even grow in cold places. Cactuses may be less than 1 inch (2.5 centimeters) high or taller than a house! Cactuses have parts that help them live in dry places.

It's a fact!

The stems of the jumping cholla fall off so easily that they seem to jump on people passing by!

The thick, fleshy **stem** holds water inside the plant.

The stem's waxy **skin** keeps water from escaping into the air.

Living stone plants grow in the deserts of South Africa. As their name suggests, they look just like small rocks!

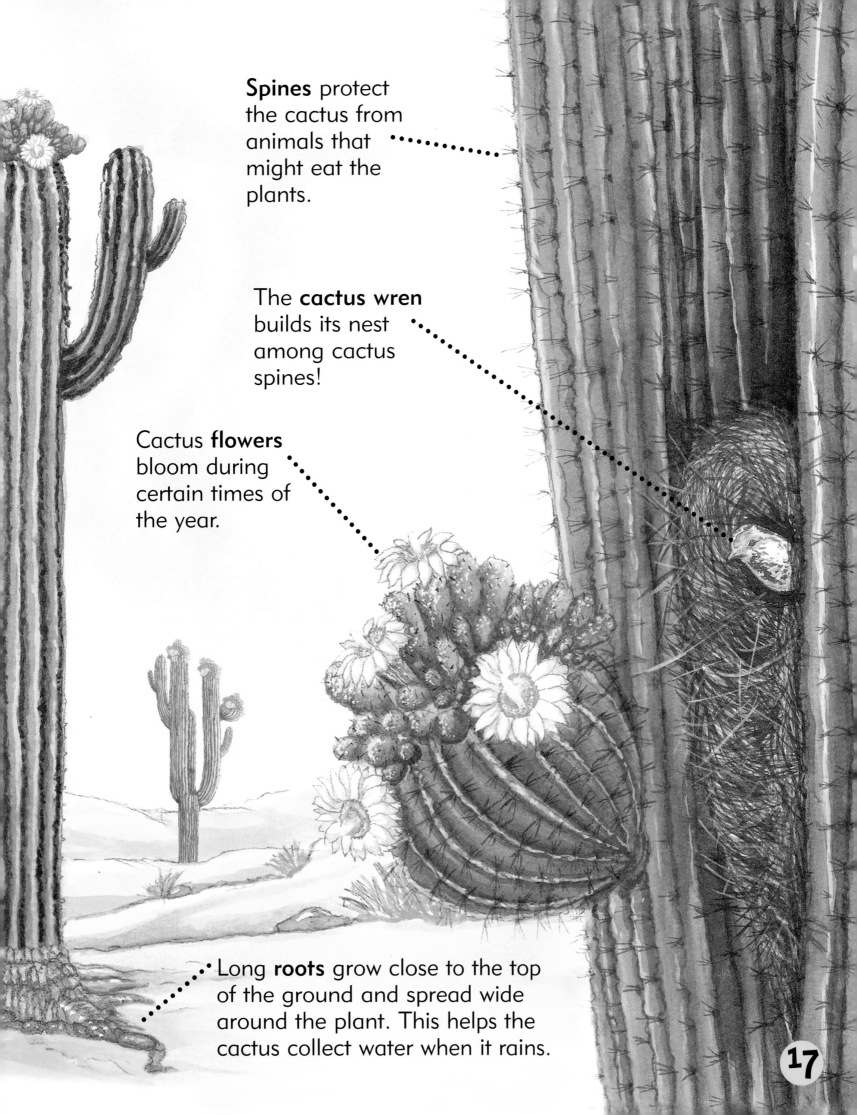

Spines protect the cactus from animals that might eat the plants.

The **cactus wren** builds its nest among cactus spines!

Cactus **flowers** bloom during certain times of the year.

Long **roots** grow close to the top of the ground and spread wide around the plant. This helps the cactus collect water when it rains.

Orchid

The orchid (*AWR kihd*) is known for its beautiful flowers. Many kinds of orchids do not grow in soil. Instead, they grow on other plants. They take the water and other things they need for food from the air or from dead plant matter near their roots. The big picture shows a comet orchid.

This **moth** has a very long "tongue" that can reach inside the flower. It drinks a sugary liquid called nectar.

It's a fact!

Vanilla flavoring comes from a kind of orchid.

The **comet orchid** grows in the rain forests of Madagascar.

The **petals** are the largest part of most flowers.

Bromeliads *(broh MEE lee adz)* are plants that grow in tropical forests. They grow mainly on other plants.

Long **tubes** hold the comet orchid's nectar.

19

Venus's-flytrap

Venus's-flytrap is a plant that eats insects! When an insect brushes against one of the hairs inside the leaf, the leaf's two parts snap shut, trapping the insect. The leaves make a fluid that helps break down the insect. Venus's-flytrap grows in wet areas along the coasts of North Carolina and South Carolina in the United States.

An **insect** is trapped inside the leaf.

The sundew is another type of meat-eating plant. It produces a sticky fluid on its leaves that traps insects.

The edges of each lobe are covered with sharp **bristles**.

Small, white **flowers** grow at the end of a **stalk**.

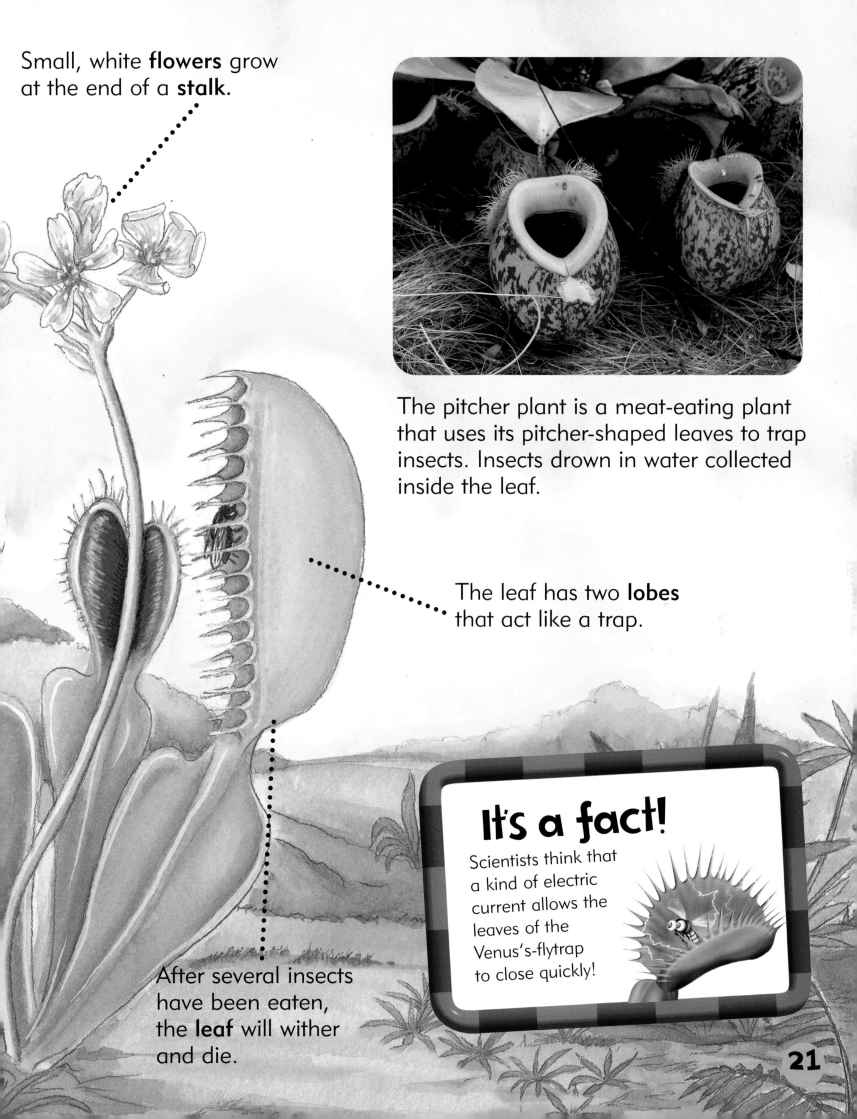

The pitcher plant is a meat-eating plant that uses its pitcher-shaped leaves to trap insects. Insects drown in water collected inside the leaf.

The leaf has two **lobes** that act like a trap.

After several insects have been eaten, the **leaf** will wither and die.

It's a fact!

Scientists think that a kind of electric current allows the leaves of the Venus's-flytrap to close quickly!

How plants help us

Without plants, people could not survive. Plants help to make the air we breathe. Our food comes from plants or from animals that eat plants. We also make many useful things from plants. The big picture shows some of the things we get from plants.

Fruits and vegetables are healthy foods that come from plants.

Wood from trees is used to make furniture, houses, and paper.

Milk and **meat** come from animals that eat plants.

Grains are used to make bread and many other foods for people and animals.

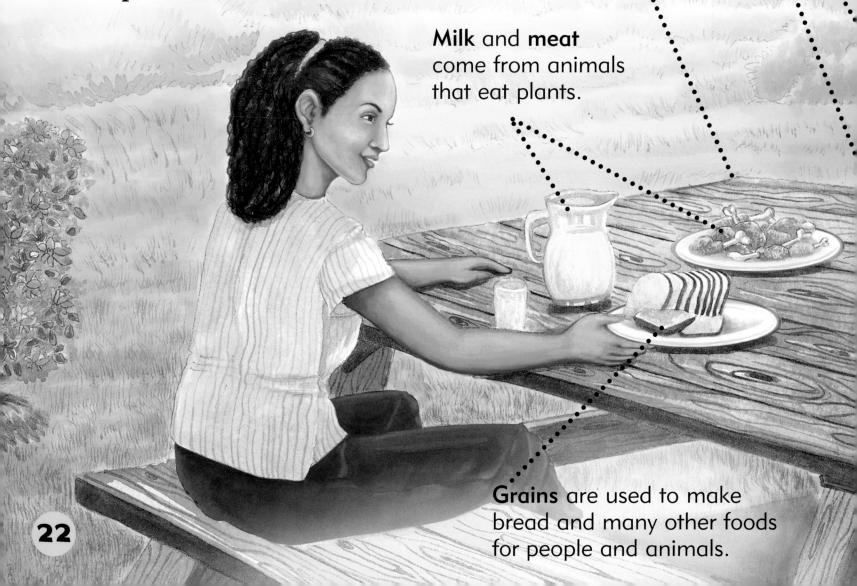

Clothing is made from cotton and other plants.

Certain kinds of aloe plants have a special juice inside their leaves. The juice can be used to treat burns.

It's a fact!

Many kinds of medicine come from plants. People discovered the main ingredient for aspirin in the bark of a willow tree.

23

Greenhouse growing

People can grow plants all year in a greenhouse. Its roof and walls are made of clear glass or plastic so that plenty of sunlight gets through. A greenhouse can be heated so that plants are kept warm. Flowers, vegetables, and other kinds of plants can grow in a greenhouse.

Words you know

Here are some words that you learned earlier. Say them out loud, then try to find the things in the picture.

spines   cactus   tree

stem   skin   flower

Which plants have leaves?

Which plants have flowers?

25

Did you know?

The rafflesia is the world's largest flower. It can measure over 3 feet (90 centimeters) across. It smells like rotting meat!

The banyan tree spreads by growing trunklike roots from its branches. In time, a banyan may cover acres of ground!

The ginkgo tree is a member of a group of plants that lived millions of years ago. It was eaten by dinosaurs!

The comet orchid has very long tubes that hold the flower's sugary liquid. Only one kind of moth has a "tongue" long enough to drink from the tubes!

The trunks of many trees have layers that look like rings. Each ring stands for a year in the tree's life.

Some plants grow on non-living things like stones, rocks, or logs. Some may even grow on telephone wires!

Puzzles

Close-up!

We've zoomed in on parts of three different plants. Can you figure out which plants you are looking at?

1

2

3

Answers on page 32.

Chow down!

Can you match each living creature to the kind of plant it likes to eat? Follow the lines to find out!

human being   panda   cow

grass   apple   bamboo

Match up!

Match each word on the left with its picture on the right.

1. orchid

2. cactus

3. Venus's-flytrap

4. fern

5. grass

6. aloe

a

b

c

d

e

f

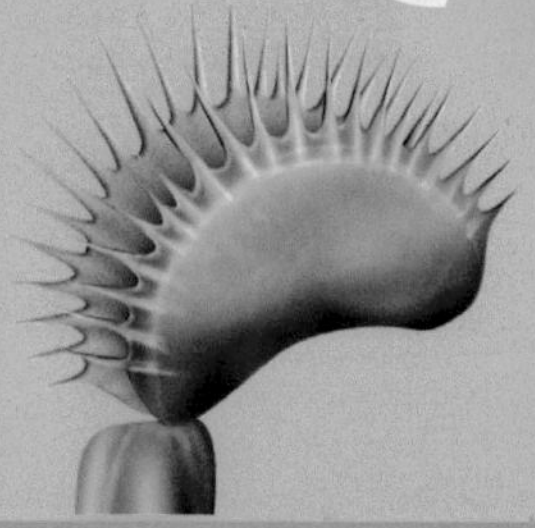

Answers on page 32.

True or false

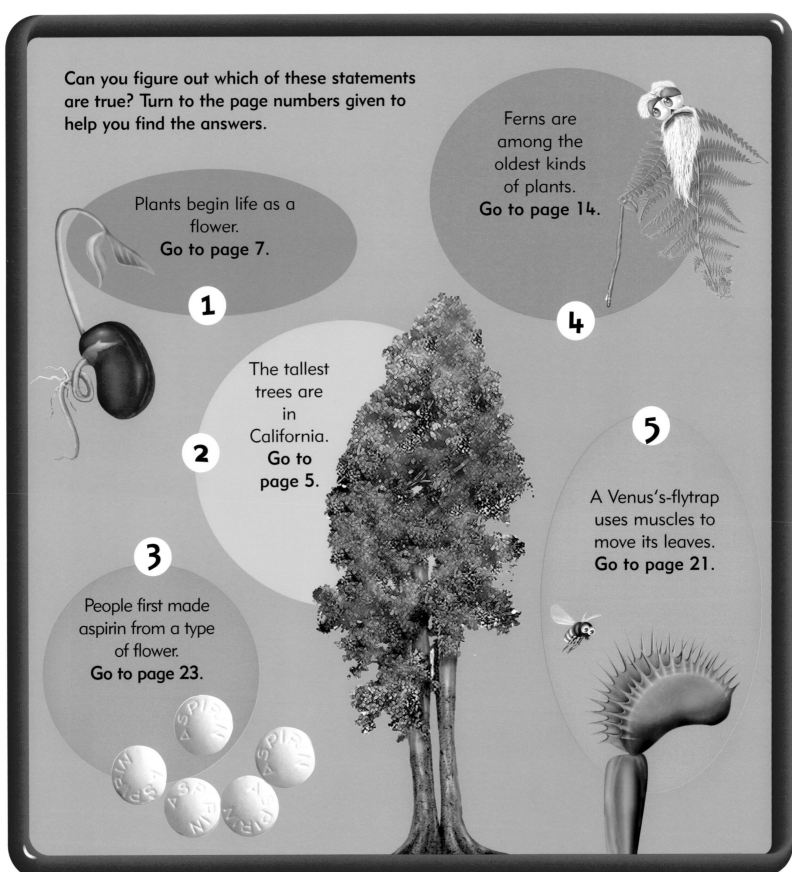

Can you figure out which of these statements are true? Turn to the page numbers given to help you find the answers.

1 Plants begin life as a flower. **Go to page 7.**

2 The tallest trees are in California. **Go to page 5.**

3 People first made aspirin from a type of flower. **Go to page 23.**

4 Ferns are among the oldest kinds of plants. **Go to page 14.**

5 A Venus's-flytrap uses muscles to move its leaves. **Go to page 21.**

Answers on page 32.

Find out more

Books

Amazing Plants by Honor Head (Gareth Stevens, 2008)
This book includes information about some unusual and fascinating plants—from meat-eating pitcher plants to coconut palm trees.

Growing Things by Ting and Neil Morris (Sea-To-Sea, 2007)
This book includes 11 craft ideas for gardening projects.

I Like Plants! by Mary Dodson Wade (Enslow Publishers, 2009), six volumes
How does a seed become a plant? Books in this series include information about the life cycle of plants, where plants live, what plants are used for, and more.

Lively Plant Science Projects by Ann Benbow and Colin Mably (Enslow Publishers, 2009)
Includes 10 experiments with step-by-step directions.

What Do Roots Do? by Kathleen V. Kudlinski (Northword Books, 2005)
Go underground to discover the wonders of roots and all the amazing things they do for trees and plants.

Web sites

Gardening with Children
http://www.bbc.co.uk/gardening/gardening_with_children/
Indoor and outdoor family activities for hands-on learning about plants.

The Great Plant Escape
http://urbanext.illinois.edu/gpe/
Six "case studies," with problems to solve and experiments to make, help readers discover the importance of plants.

Grow a Bean Buddy
http://gardens.si.edu/horticulture/res_ed/beanbuddyactivity.pdf
A gardening activity that teaches about the basic parts and needs of plants, from the Smithsonian Institution.

My First Garden
http://urbanext.illinois.edu/firstgarden/l
This family activity gives you a chance to help birds build their nests.

Answers

Puzzles
from pages 28 and 29

Close-up!
1. Venus's-flytrap
2. cactus
3. fern

Match up!
1. e
2. a
3. f
4. d
5. b
6. c

True or false
from page 30

1. false
2. true
3. false
4. true
5. false

Index